The Robber's Mask

By **Carol Krueger**

Illustrated by **Suzie Byrne**

The Robber's Mask

William and Megan Thomas called their dog, Cassie. She loved bringing things home. She'd collect all kinds of stuff – shoes, toys, items from people's rubbish bags, and even socks.

Cassie adored socks, and she kept turning up with them – striped ones, red ones, ones with holes, yellow ones, lacy ones, dirty ones, and even smelly ones.

"Disgusting!" said Megan, looking at the pile of socks Cassie had collected.

"We should put up a *Lost Property* sign on the front lawn!" said Dad.

"Well, what do you expect from a golden retriever!" grinned William. "She's just retrieving things!"

Clarify: **retrieving**

- A finding
- B slobbering on
- C bringing back

A, B or C?

One day, Cassie brought home something that gave Megan the shivers. It was a mask. A black, knitted mask with holes cut out for the eyes and mouth!

"Yuck!" said Megan, picking it up. "It looks like a robber's mask."

"Get real!" said William. "You've been watching too much TV!"

"But who would wear a mask like this?" Megan asked.

"Maybe someone who was feeling cold," said William.

"Yeah, right! It's the middle of spring!" Megan argued.

"Yeah, right!"

Question:

Why do you think Megan thought the mask was a robber's mask?

Megan put down the mask and picked up the TV remote. She flicked from Channel Two to Channel Three, and pressed record as her favourite programme began.

"Hey!" yelled William. "That's my videotape, and I don't want your dumb programme on it!"

"Get lost!" said Megan.

William grabbed the remote off her and changed the channel.

A news reporter appeared on the screen, announcing a bank robbery.

"That's Mum's bank!" said Megan. She felt a strange tingle. It crept up her spine like a long-legged spider. The TV flashed pictures of the bank robbers caught on security cameras. They were wearing masks ... just like the one Cassie had brought home.

Simile:

A simile is a group of words that helps the reader draw a mind picture. It uses the word *like* or *as* to make a comparison.

Can you find a simile?

Megan realised that she had taped the news. She rewound the tape and pressed the play button. "Hey, Mum! Come and watch this!" she shouted.

Mum watched the news, and Megan showed her the mask. "Look!" she said. "It's the same mask. The robbers were wearing this mask."

"It does look like the same mask," said Mum.

"Ring the police!" said Megan.

"I will," said Mum. "Don't let Cassie get that mask! We'll need to show it to the police."

Predict:

What do you think might happen in the story now?

?

Just before dinner, a police officer came to the door. Cassie barked at her and slobbered over her shoes.

"Mrs Thomas?" said the officer. "My name is Officer Wong. I've come to look at the mask. Where did your dog get it from?"

"I don't know," said Mum. "Cassie brings stuff home all the time. I think she gets it from around the neighbourhood."

Cassie barked loudly.

"Then this mask was probably found somewhere near here," said Officer Wong. "I'll take it down to the station."

Megan watched as Officer Wong drove off. Cassie followed the police car for a few metres, then she came back with a ball from next door.

Synonym:

A word or phrase with a similar meaning to another word or phrase.

Which word is the synonym for slobbered?

A   nibbled

B   licked

C   dribbled

A, B or C?

11

Later that night, Megan noticed something strange. There was a light coming from the burnt-out house next door. No one had lived there for months.

She went to get William. "There's a light coming from that burnt house!" she said.

William got up from the computer and looked out the window.

"That's freaky!" he said.

Megan felt that strange tingle creep up her spine again. "I wonder what's going on?" she said. "Let's tell Mum!"

Inference:

... no one had lived there for months.

What inferences can you make about the light coming from the burnt-out house?

... a light coming from the burnt-out house

Megan and William followed Mum across the back lawn. Cassie came, too, barking loudly.

But the light in the house had gone off. The house was now just a shadow against the night sky.

"That's odd!" said Mum.

"Maybe you just imagined it!"

Then Cassie started digging. She covered everyone in dirt.

"Cassie!" they yelled.

She retrieved a buried shoe and gave it to Mum. "Thanks, Cassie!" she said sarcastically.

Cassie didn't listen. She just trotted back inside.

the light in the house had gone off

The next day, William and Megan were taking Cassie for a walk. Suddenly, she yanked on her lead and raced down a drive into the burnt house.

"Cassie, come back!" Megan yelled. She waited ... she didn't want to go inside that house. She yelled again. "Cassie, come back!"

"Go in and get her!" said William.

"Why can't you go?" Megan replied.

"Are you scared?"

"I'll go – but you have to come, too!" said William.

Megan followed William reluctantly.

. . . Cassie, come back!

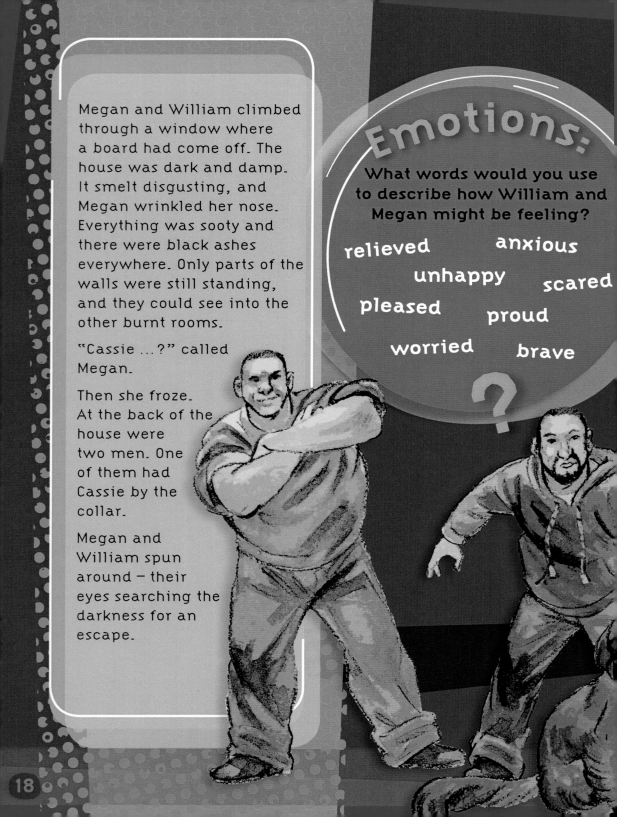

Megan and William climbed through a window where a board had come off. The house was dark and damp. It smelt disgusting, and Megan wrinkled her nose. Everything was sooty and there were black ashes everywhere. Only parts of the walls were still standing, and they could see into the other burnt rooms.

"Cassie ...?" called Megan.

Then she froze. At the back of the house were two men. One of them had Cassie by the collar.

Megan and William spun around – their eyes searching the darkness for an escape.

Emotions:

What words would you use to describe how William and Megan might be feeling?

relieved
anxious
unhappy
scared
pleased
proud
worried
brave

?

searching the darkness

"Not so fast!" snarled one of the men. They rushed forward and grabbed Megan and William. Megan tried to scream, but she felt a sweaty hand slide over her mouth.

"You robbed that bank!" said William to the man. "We've got your mask."

"Smart kid!" the man said.

He dragged William along the dark hallway. Megan was pulled behind him. Cassie was gone.

"Please let us go, we won't say anything!" said William.

"No, you won't!" said the man. "We're going to fix it so you can't!"

... we're going to fix it so you can't!

Setting:

What words would you use to describe the setting?

a peaceful

b frightening

c tense

d happy

e gloomy

f dark

g cheerful

h bright

William felt his blood go cold. He was frightened. He couldn't breathe. His heart thumped in his chest.

Suddenly, the door crashed open and a voice shouted, "Police! Let them go!"

William and Megan saw Officer Wong standing in the hall. They wriggled free from the men's grip and raced through the open doorway.

The police rushed in. Megan and William could hear their loud footsteps crashing through the house.

Then, in a few minutes, the police came out with the men. They put them in the police car and drove away.

. . . Police! Let them go

Action and Consequence:

ACTION	CONSEQUENCE
The door crashed open	?

Can you find another action and consequence?

Officer Wong came to Megan and William's house. "We will need to take a statement," she said.

"How did you know where to find us?" asked Megan.

"Your dog told us!" said Officer Wong. "A bank worker identified the mask, and we came to search the neighbourhood. Cassie led us straight to you – and the robbers!"

"Clever Cassie!" Megan said. "You're a great retriever!"

"Clever Cassie!"

... how did you know where to find us?

Clarify:
statement

A   account of events

B   request

C   test

A, B or C?

Cassie was a hero. She was in the newspapers and on the TV.

The next day, Officer Wong came to visit. She gave Cassie a souvenir to add to her collection — a police hat!

Summary:

What key points would you put in a summary of _The Robber's Mask_?

- Megan and William had a dog called Cassie, who brought home a strange mask.
- Megan flicked from Channel Two to Channel Three.
- Megan and William saw a similar mask in a bank robbery on the TV news.
- Mum rang the police, and they came and took the mask.
- Cassie slobbered on the police officer's shoe.
- The next day, Cassie led Megan and William into a burnt-out house.
- There was black soot and ashes everywhere.
- The bank robbers were inside the house, and they grabbed Megan and William.
- Cassie escaped and led the police to the house.
- The robbers were arrested by the police.

Think about the Text

What connections can you make to the emotions, situations or characters in *The Robber's Mask*?

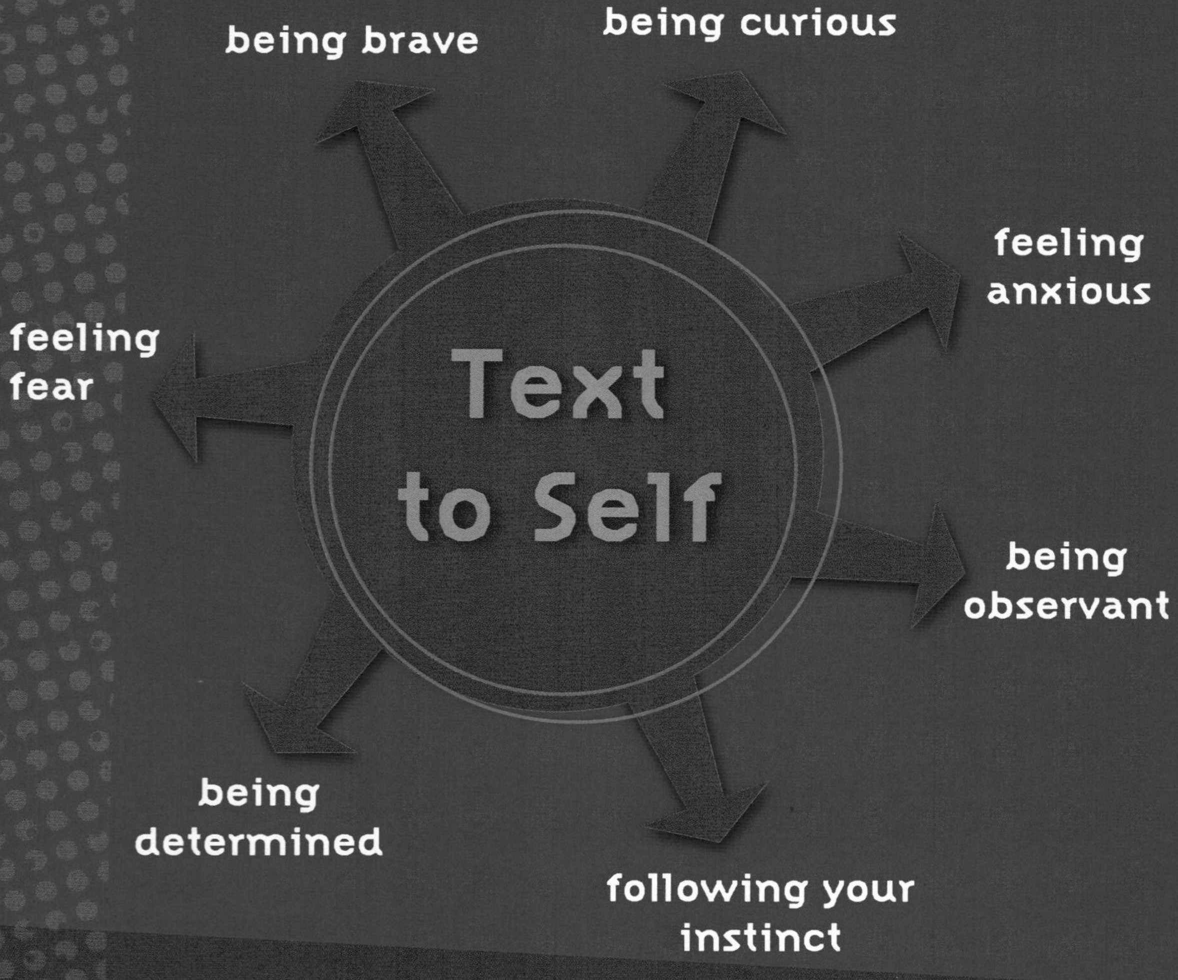

being brave

being curious

feeling anxious

feeling fear

Text to Self

being observant

being determined

following your instinct

Text to Text

Talk about other stories you may have read that have similar features. Compare the stories.

Text to World

Talk about situations in the world that might connect to elements in the story.

Planning a Narrative

1 Decide on a storyline that has an introduction, a problem and a solution

INTRODUCTION	PROBLEM	SOLUTION
William and Megan had a dog called Cassie, who brought home a robber's mask.	William and Megan got caught by bank robbers when they followed Cassie into a burnt-out house.	Cassie escaped and led the police to William, Megan, and the robbers.

2 Think about the characters and how they will think, feel and act

MEGAN

WILLIAM

CASSIE

MUM

THE ROBBERS

3 Decide on the setting

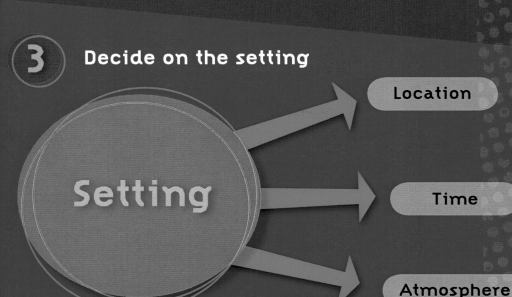

Setting

- Location
- Time
- Atmosphere

4 Think about events in order of sequence

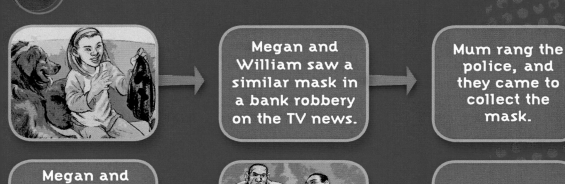

Megan and William saw a similar mask in a bank robbery on the TV news.

Mum rang the police, and they came to collect the mask.

Megan and William took Cassie for a walk, and she ran off into a burnt-out house.

Cassie escaped and led the police to the house.

Narratives usually ...

 have an introduction that quickly tells:
  - who the story is about
  - where the story is set
  - when the story happened

 have a problem that creates excitement and makes the reader want to read on to find out how the problem is solved

create an emotional response within the reader

include description and dialogue

create mood and tension

 include characters, setting and mood that are connected to create a believable storyline